PHONICS Workbook

LEVEL 2

Published in Moonstone
by Rupa Publications India Pvt. Ltd 2022
7/16, Ansari Road, Daryaganj
New Delhi 110002

Sales centres:
Allahabad Bengaluru Chennai
Hyderabad Jaipur Kathmandu
Kolkata Mumbai

Copyright © Rupa Publications India Pvt. Ltd 2022

The views and opinions expressed in this book are
the authors' own and the facts are as reported by them
which have been verified to the extent possible,
and the publishers are not in any way liable for the same.

All rights reserved.
No part of this publication may be reproduced, transmitted,
or stored in a retrieval system, in any form or by any means,
electronic, mechanical, photocopying, recording or otherwise,
without the prior permission of the publisher.

P-ISBN: 978-93-5520-644-2
E-ISBN: 978-93-5520-645-9

First impression 2022

10 9 8 7 6 5 4 3 2 1

The moral right of the authors has been asserted.

Printed in India
This book is sold subject to the condition that it shall not,
by way of trade or otherwise, be lent, resold, hired out, or otherwise
circulated, without the publisher's prior consent, in any form of binding
or cover other than that in which it is published.

Contents

Beginning Sounds..................... 4
Final Sounds......................... 5
Let's Play Detective 6
Odd One Out 7
Making Words 8
Short Vowel A 9
Word Bank 10
Story Time Activity 11
Missing Sounds 12
Picture Reading 13
Short Vowel E....................... 14
Word Bank 15
Story Time Activity 16
Where are the Consonants? 17
Picture Reading..................... 18
Short Vowel I 19
Word Bank 20
Story Time Activity 21
Let's Make Words 22
Picture Reading..................... 23
Short Vowel O 24

Word Bank 25
Story Time Activity 26
Word Wall 27
Picture Reading..................... 28
Short Vowel U 29
Word Bank 30
Story Time Activity 31
Spell and Write 32
Picture Reading..................... 33
Word Search........................ 34
Missing Sounds 35
See, Say, Spell and Write 36
Rhyming Words 37
Rhyme Time......................... 38
Story Time Activity 39
I Can Read 40
Bear Hunting 41
Articles-A and An 42
Weaving Words 46
Let's Revise-1...................... 47
Let's Revise-2...................... 48

Beginning Sounds

Match the beginning sound to the correct picture.

4

Final Sounds

Look at each object and say its name. Write the missing letter sound to complete the name.

Bu......  Duc......

Ha......  Hipp......

Ma......  Su......

Bo......  An......

Lea......  Le......

Sta......  Dru......

Let's Play Detective

How many letters can you spot?

Odd One Out

Look at the pictures and say the names of the objects aloud. Now circle the object whose name starts with a different sound.

|  Fish |  Baby |  Ball |  Bat |

|  Man |  Meal |  Jam |  Mop |

|  Drum |  Dog | 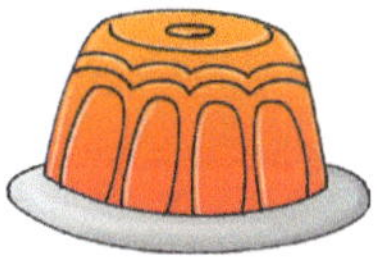 Jelly |  Day |

| 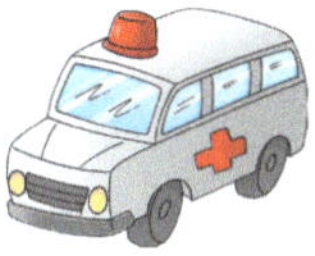 Ambulance |  Ant |  Spider |  Arrow |

|  Ice Cream |  Igloo |  Iguana | 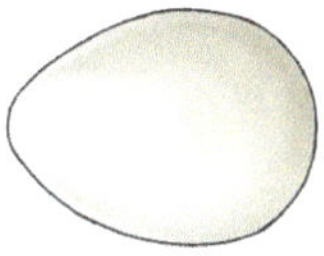 Egg |

|  Nest |  Nap |  Butterfly |  Night |

Making Words

Connect the letters to form the correct spelling, and then trace the spellings.

s	h	p
a	k	y

sky

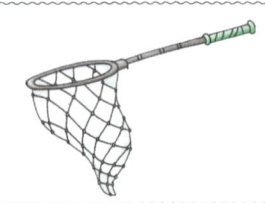

y	r	t
n	e	j

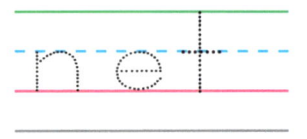
net

b	o	p
a	g	q

bag

s	d	p
a	o	g

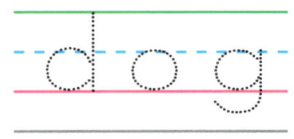
dog

m	h	n
c	a	e

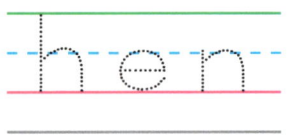
hen

p	i	c
s	n	h

pin

p	o	i
m	a	d

mad

Short Vowel A

Read the story. Repeat the words in red. Can you hear the a sound in these words?

It is a sunny day. Everyone is watching a cricket match. The player has a bat. He has hit the ball with his bat. A man runs after the ball.

A fat man wearing a hat is enjoying the match. A woman with a cat and a lad is with him. The cat is looking at a rat. The woman has a bag on her lap.

Word Bank

Let's read aloud a few short a vowel words.

ab	cab, dab, lab, nab, tab
ad	bad, had, lad, mad, pad, sad
ag	bag, nag, tag, rag, wag
am	dam, ham, jam, ram, yam
an	can, van, ran, fan, man, tan, pan
ap	cap, gap, lap, map, nap, tap
as	gas, has, was
at	fat, hat, pat, sat, mat, rat, fat, bat
ax	fax, tax, wax, axe

Story Time Activity

Read the following sentences and underline the words which have the short a sound.

Sam is a cat.

Rap is a rat.

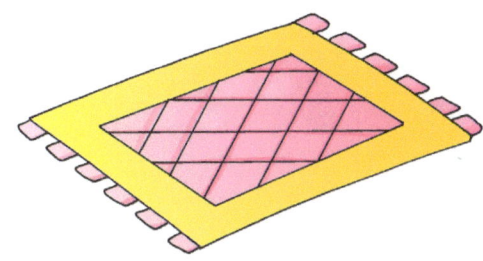

Sam sat on a mat.

Rap sat on a can.

Sam and Rap play on the mat.

They ate the jam.
Mom was sad.

Sam and Rap had a nap under the fan.

Missing Sounds

Say the name of each picture aloud. Write the missing sound.

 Ha......

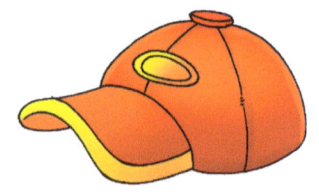 C......p

 ......am

 ......an

 Ta......

 ......ab

 R......t

 Ma......

 Sa......

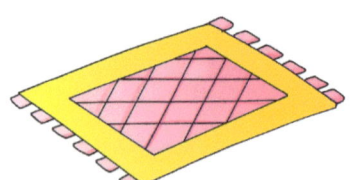 ......at

Picture Reading

Match the phrase with the correct picture.

Phrase	Picture
A lazy lad	
An old hat	
A little rat	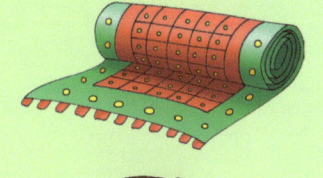
A big mat	
A fat man	
A red van	

Short Vowel E

Read the story. Repeat the words in red. Can you hear the e sound in these words?

Ted has hurt his leg. He is lying in the garden on a bed. He is wearing a red shirt. He has three pets, Greg the dog, Ped the frog, and Meg the hen. Meg helps Ted by laying eggs. Ted's friend Ben helps Ted by selling Meg's eggs. Ped helps Ted. He cleans the well with a net. Greg loves to eat eggs. 'Look Ben!' says Ted, 'Up in the sky is a jet.'

Word Bank

Let's read a few short e vowel words.

eck	deck, neck, peck, wreck
ed	bed, fed, led, red, wed
eg	beg, keg, leg, peg
et	let, met, net, pet, wet
en	den, hen, men, pen, ten
ell	bell, fell, well, smell, tell

Story Time Activity

Read the following story and underline the words which have the short e sound.

This is my pet. Her name is Meg.

Meg smells the eggs.

Mummy feeds her eggs.

And Meg makes a mess.

Meg has a friend. His name is Ben. Meg and Ben play all day.

Where are the Consonants?

Look at the object and write its beginning and ending sound.

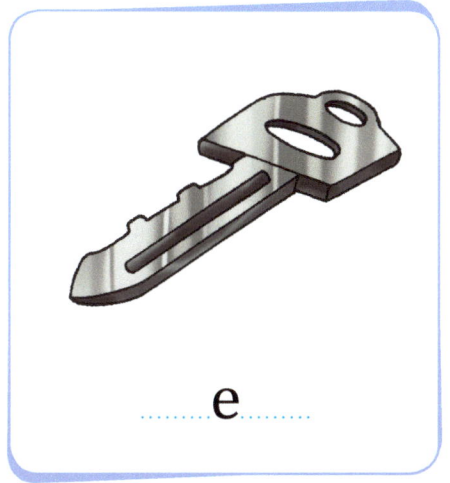
__k__ e __y__

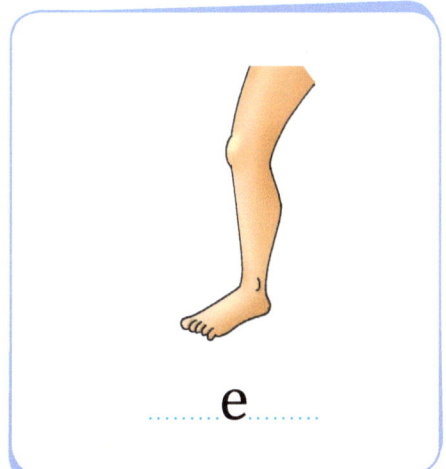
__l__ e __g__

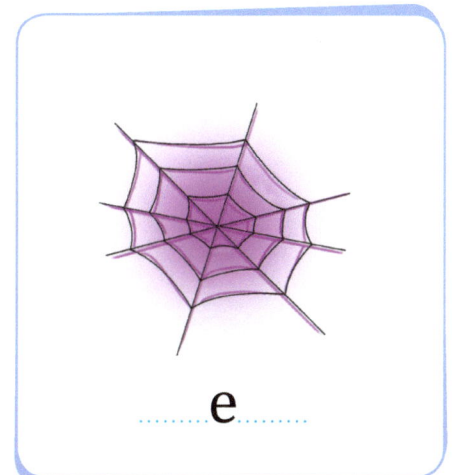
__w__ e __b__

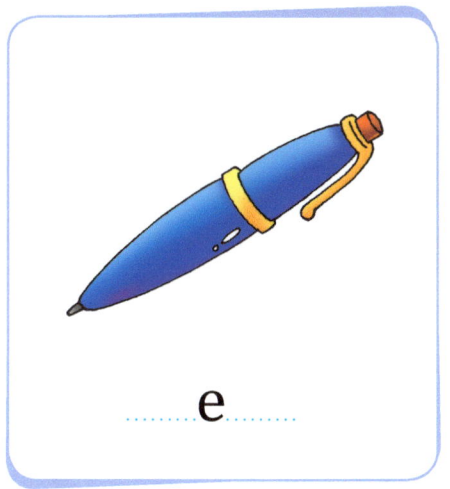
__p__ e __n__

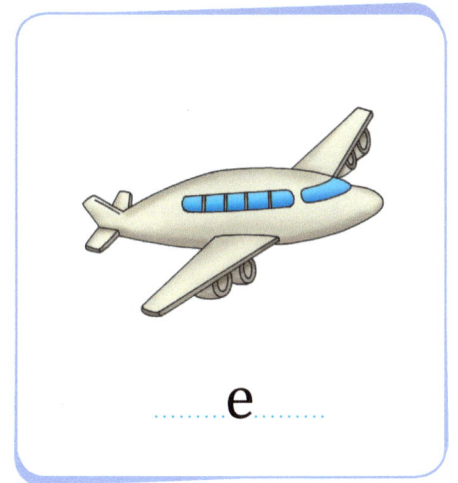
__j__ e __t__

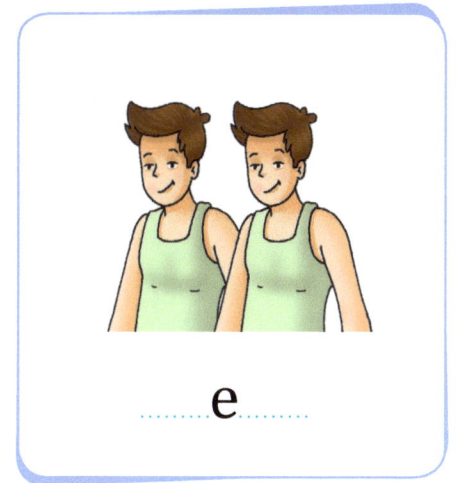
__m__ e __n__

__h__ e __n__

__b__ e __d__

__d__ e __n__

Picture Reading

Match the phrase with the picture.

Phrase	Picture
A fat hen	
A red pen	
A big tent	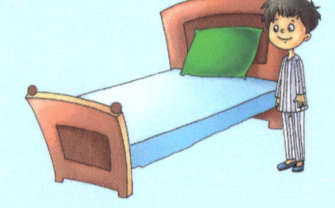
A wet cat	
A small bed	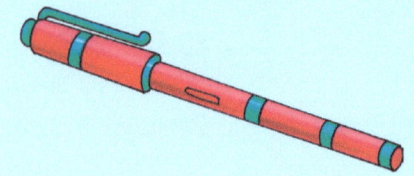

Short Vowel I

Read the story. Repeat the words in red. Can you hear the short i sound in these words?

Tim is a big kid. He likes to wear a wig. He has two friends, Jim and Bill.

Jim and Bill are twins. Both like to sing.

Jim and Bill are at Tim's house. 'Tim, you are sick. Let's take you to the doctor quickly,' says Jim.

Word Bank

Let's read a few short i vowel words.

ib	bib, nib, fib, rib
id	lid, bid, kid, rid, did
ig	wig, big, pig, dig, jig
in	bin, tin, pin, win, fin
ink	pink, sink, wink, link
it	lit, pit, hit, kit

Story Time Activity

Read the following story and underline the words which have short i sound.

Billy was a little boy. He wished to be in a band. But he only had a little tin can and a big pan. Billy hit the big pan. 'Ting-ting-ting,' it began to ring. Billy jiggled the tin can. 'Jingle-jingle,' came the sound.

'Jingle jingle! Ting-ting-ting', the pan and the can began to sing. Billy did a little jig out of joy.

Let's Make Words

Choose a consonant from the box below and add it at the beginning of the groups of letters to form meaningful words. Match the word with the correct picture.

D	F	F	T	S	W	K

ix	....	
ig	....	
id	....	
ip	....	
in	....	
it	....	
ig	....	

22

Picture Reading

Match the phrase with the correct picture.

Phrase	Picture
Dig a pit	
A big tin	
Eat a fig	
Sit and eat	
A pink fish	
A dirty bin	

Short Vowel O

Read the story aloud. Repeat the words in red. Can you hear the short o sound in these words?

Long ago in Tokyo there lived Mary Jo. She had a toy room in her house. It had many toys. Her favourite toy was Pinocchio. Mary Jo played all day. One day she lost her yo-yo. She looked everywhere but found it nowhere. Mary Jo sobbed hard. The next day she lost her spinning top. Oh how she hoped to get her toys back! At last she spotted them on the top of a box.

Word Bank

Let's read a few short o vowel words.

ob	mob, sob, rob, job
od	cod, pod, rod, nod, god
og	dog, fog, log, frog, jog
op	top, mop, hop, pop, shop
ot	dot, cot, hot, pot, lot, got, rot
ox	ox, fox, box, pox

Story Time Activity

Read the following story and underline the words with the short vowel o sound.

This is Tom.
Tom is a little boy.

This is Rob.
Rob is Tom's pet dog.

Tom takes Rob for a walk.

Rob sees a pot.
He does not touch the pot,
because it is hot.

Tom has a toy. It is a top.
Tom and Rob play with the top.

Word Wall

Complete the word wall. One has been done for you.

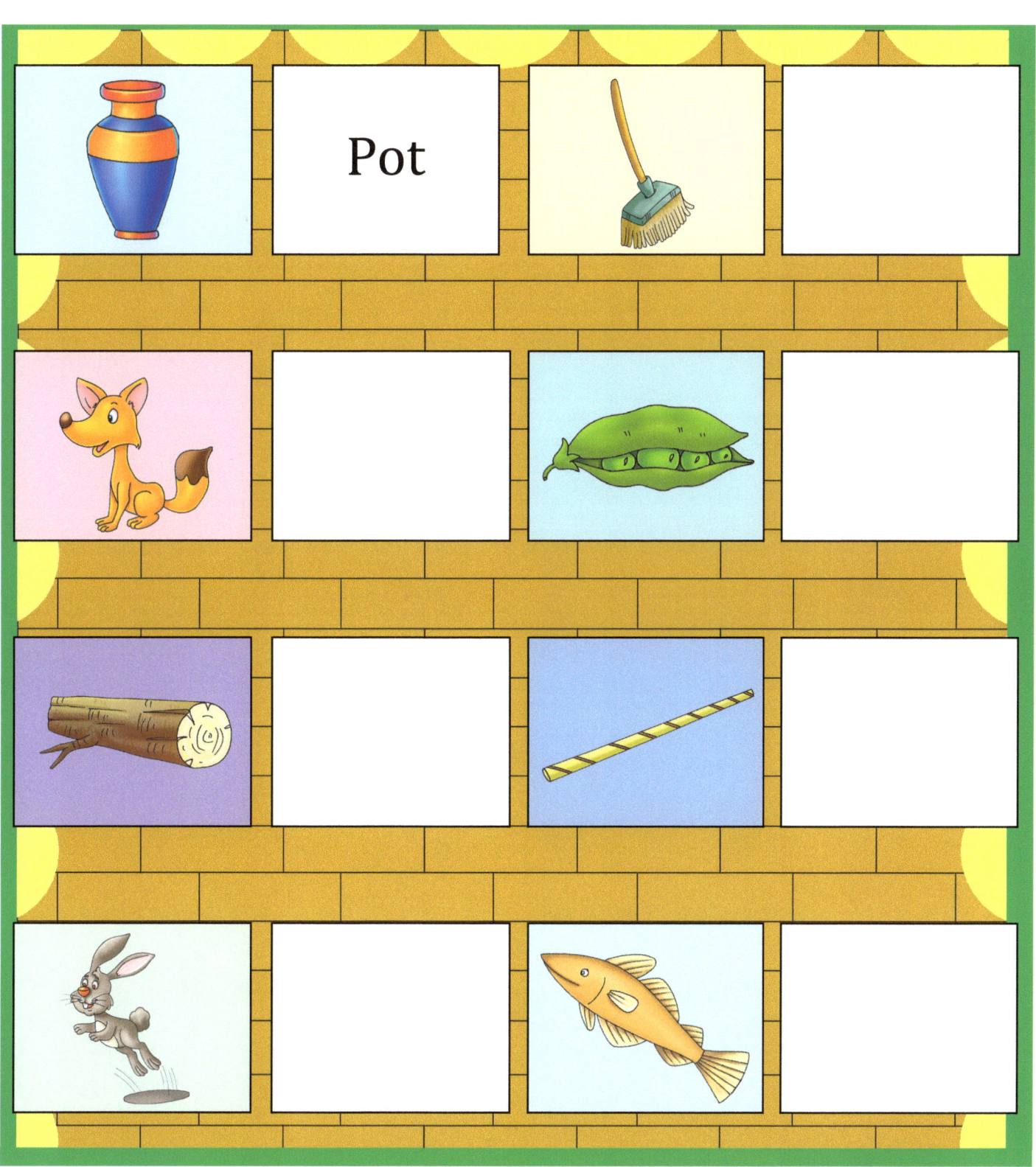

Picture Reading

Match the phrase with the picture.

Phrase	Picture
A boy with toy	
A hot pot	
A boy on a log	
A big dot	
A cop with a rod	

Short Vowel U

Read the story. Repeat the words in red. Can you hear the short u sound in these words?

The pug, the cub and the pup are friends.

They live in the pug's hut.

The cub has a cup.

The pup has a jug.

They all sit on a rug.

They play in the mud and have fun.

They give each other hugs.

Word Bank

Let's read some short u vowel words.

| ub | cub, tub, rub, club, hub, scrub |

| ug | hug, bug, dug, jug, mug, rug |

| un | bun, sun, gun, fun, run |

| up | up, cup, pup, yup, tup |

| ut | cut, hut, but, nut |

Story Time Activity

Read the following sentences and circle the words that have the short u sound.

Look at the hot sun.

Do not run.

Get into the hut.

Sit on a rug.

Eat the buns and the nuts.

Have your bath in the tub.

Spell and Write

Spell the words aloud and trace them.

Nut

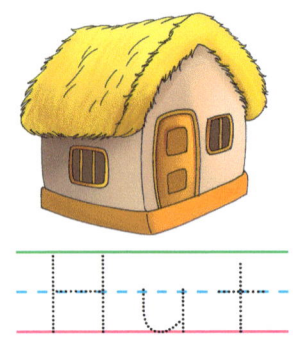
Hut

Bus

Bud

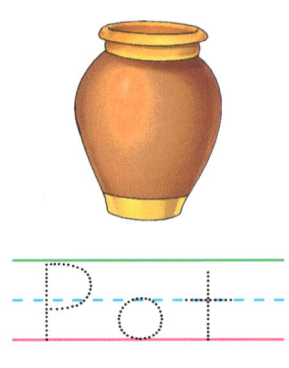
Pot

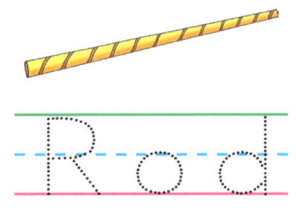
Rod

Bug

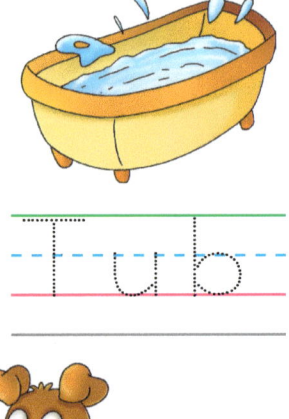
Tub

Mug

Dog

Picture Reading

Match the phrase with the picture.

Phrase	Picture
Hug a pup	
A lad with a cub	
A cop with a gun	
The hot sun	
A boy in a tub	
Have fun	

Word Search

Find the words listed in the word search puzzle below.

p	e	n	t	k	t	h	o
r	t	s	b	m	i	d	j
v	a	c	e	n	n	r	l
m	c	a	d	j	o	y	y
u	x	t	o	t	p	i	n
g	i	m	h	a	j	w	i
l	h	z	o	p	h	t	o
f	t	v	p	k	n	x	a

pen
tin
mug
tap
joy
cat
pin
hop
bed

Circle the correct word for the given pictures.

Lid

Fig

Pup

Cub

Bat

Ant

Net

Wet

Pot

Hot

Missing Sounds

Fill in the missing sounds to complete the given words.

Fa......	......ap	D......t
F......g	......eg	N......t
Gu......	P......g	......od

See, Say, Spell and Write

Look at the pictures, say the words aloud, spell them out and write them in the given spaces.

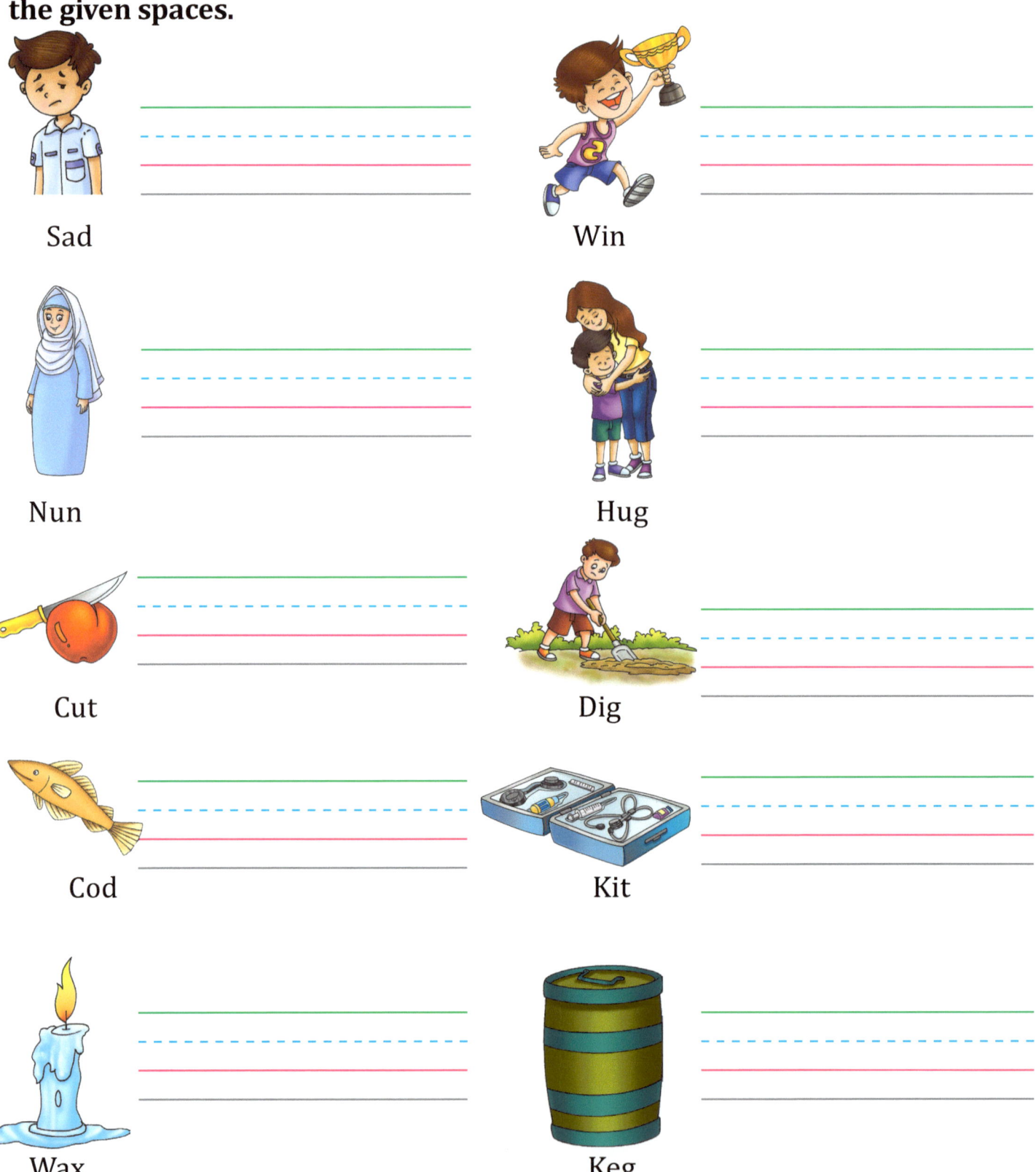

Sad

Nun

Cut

Cod

Wax

Win

Hug

Dig

Kit

Keg

Rhyming Words

Read the words aloud. Can you think of one more rhyming word for each group? Write the word in the given space.

Can	 Man	 Pan	....
 Jet	 Bed	 Red	....
 Wig	 Dig	 Fig	....
 Ox	 Fox	 Box	....
 Sun	 Bun	 Fun	....

Rhyme Time

Read and match the words that rhyme.

A	B
Tab	Dug
Fat	Cap
Let	Ten
Log	Lab
Pen	Cat
Map	Jet
Bug	Dog

Story Time Activity

Read the story and colour the vowels.

Daddy got a pet cat.

The cat sat on mummy's lap.

Jim gave it an egg.

Jane gave it some milk.

The cat ate the egg and lapped up the milk.

Then it lay down on the mat and fell asleep.

I Can Read

Read these sight words aloud.

a	this	it	who	that	if
an	the	in	and	for	us
go	on	by	so	is	to
these	be	am	those	me	my
where	he	no	with	she	

Bear Hunting

"We are going on a bear hunt!" Help the hunters find the bear. As you move along the path, read all the words and circle the vowel sounds.

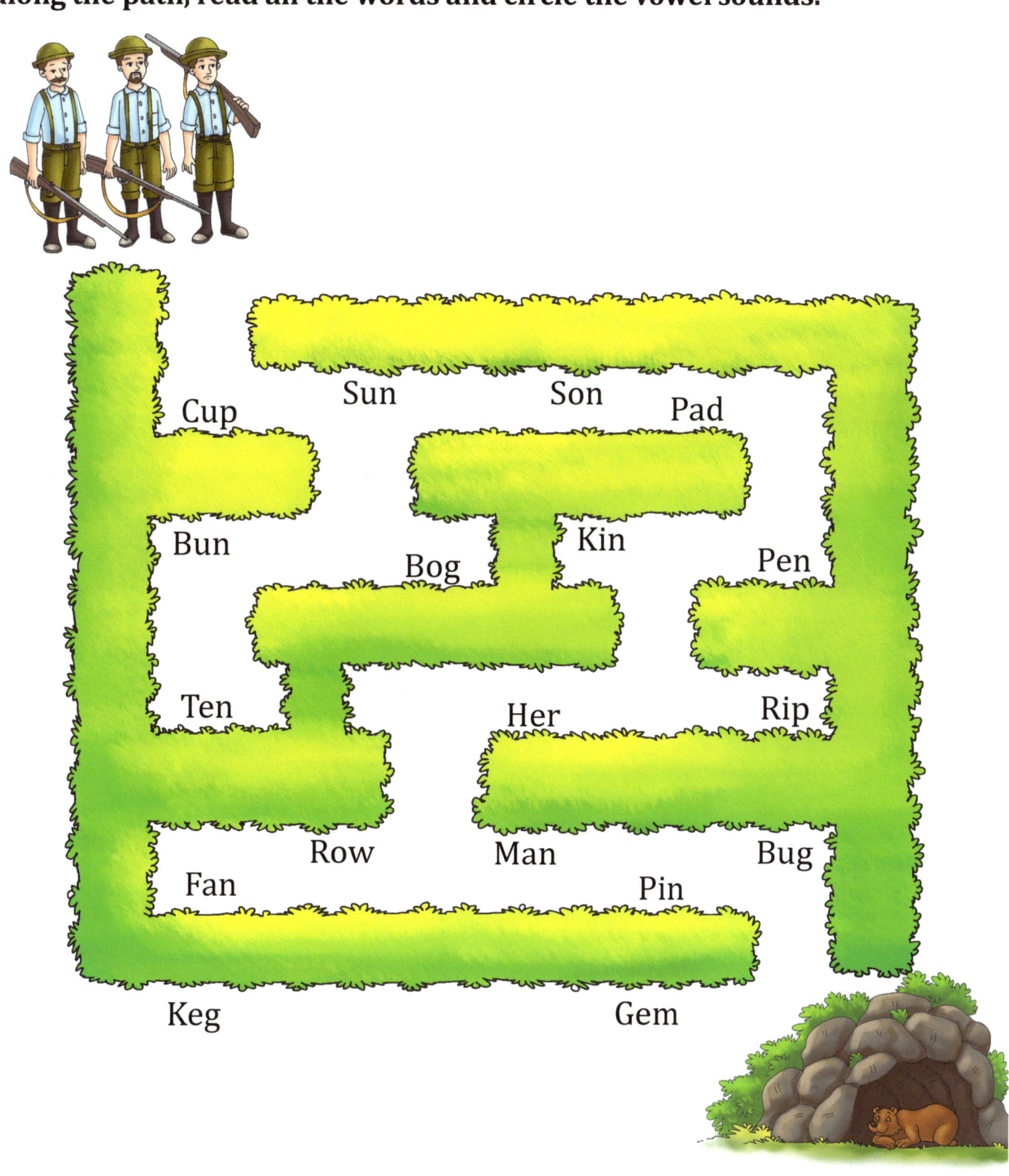

41

Articles - A and An

Write the names of the objects shown in the pictures.

An ....

An ....

A ....

A ....

A ....

A ....

Write the names of the objects shown in the pictures.

A hat

A fan

An ice cream

A barrel

A yo-yo

A net

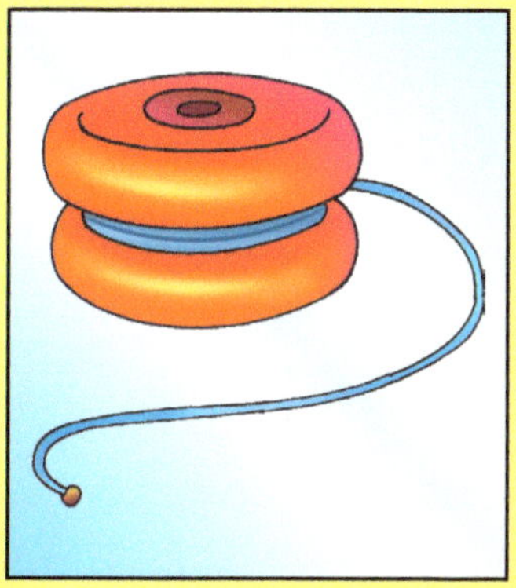

Write the names of the objects shown in the pictures.

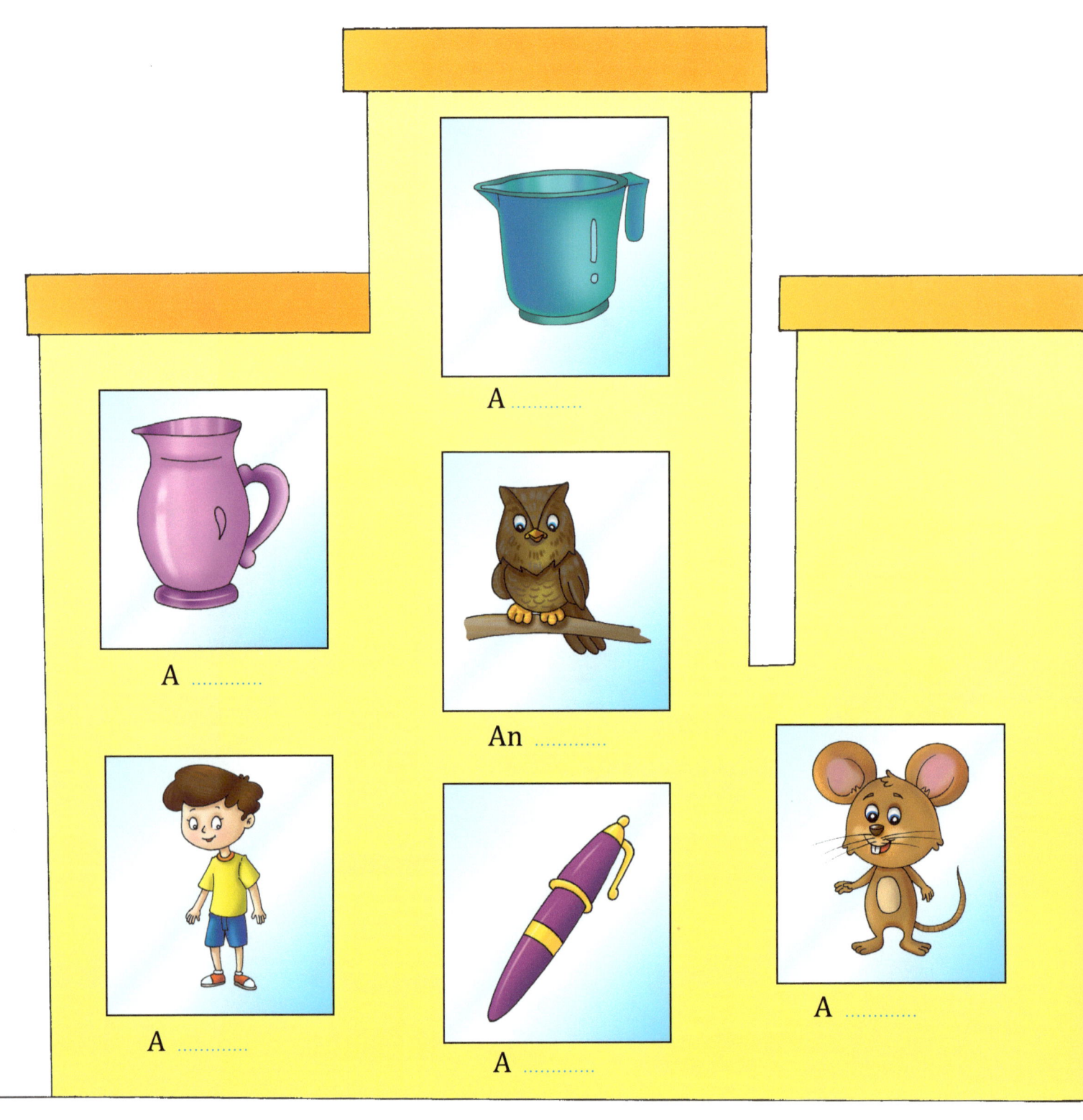

Teacher's Note:

Talk to the children about the vowels, a, e, i, o, u and the use of an with vowels and a with consonants.

A ....

An ....

A ....

A ....

A ....

A ....

Weaving Words

Look at each picture carefully. Now circle the correct letters that make up the word. Write the word in the space given.

t   b   c   a   k   p   ....

o   p   o   k   t   x   ....

h   r   e   g   n   f   ....

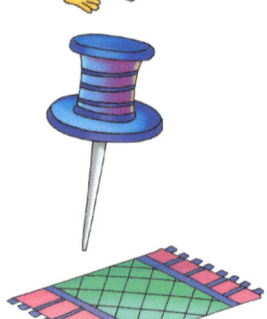
t   p   i   f   m   n   ....

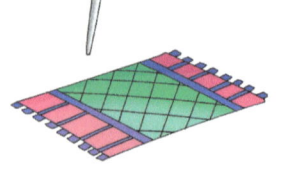
h   c   r   u   g   d   ....

g   e   c   g   g   z   ....

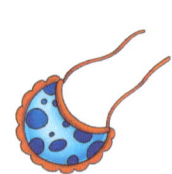
b   a   d   i   b   t   ....

a   d   s   w   a   d   ....

Let's Revise-1

Fill in the blanks with the correct sound.

A as in	ant,	....pe	and	....pple	
B as in	....all,	bat	and	....ean	
C as in	....ar,	....rab	and	crow	
D as in	deer,	....onkey	and	....og	
E as in	....ye,	egg	and	....lephant	
F as in	....lower,	fan	and	....arm	
G as in	....rass,	....oat	and	goal	
H as in	house,	....en	and	....orn	
I as in	....gloo,	ice	and	....nk	
J as in	....am,	....oker	and	jeans	
K as in	....ing,	kite	and	....ind	
L as in	long,	....ine	and	....ace	
M as in	....eat,	man	and	....ilk	
N as in	....est,	....ose	and	neck	
O as in	oil,	....range	and	....wl	
P as in	....en,	pony	and	....ond	
Q as in	....ueen,	....uiet	and	quilts	
R as in	red,	....ainbow	and	....ound	
S as in	....ong,	sail	and	....and	
T as in	....ail,	....oy	and	tent	
U as in	....mbrella,	useful	and	....nicorn	
V as in	....an,	vet	and	....ine	
W as in	....ind,	....ater	and	walk	
X as in	xylophone,	a....e	and	o....	
Y as in	....ak,	yawn	and	....o-yo	
Z as in	....ebra,	zoo	and	....ig zag	

47

Let's Revise-2

Fill in the blanks with the correct sound.

An ......ngry alligator

A ......ig balloon

A cute ......at

A dirty ......og

An eager ......mu

A ......at fish

A good ......ame

A helping ......and

An icy ......gloo

A ......am jar

A kind ......ing

A ......ong line

A mean ......an

A ......ew nail

An ......ld owl

A ......et parrot

A quiet ......ueen

A round ......at

A ......illy song

A tiny ......oad

An upset ......ncle

A vast ......alley

A ......ise wolf

An extra a......e

A yellow ......olk

A zebra in a ......oo